East Meets West

Exploration by Land

Paul Strathern

Thameside Press

Distributed in the United States by
Smart Apple Media
1980 Lookout Drive
North Mankato, MN 56003

ISBN 1-931983-32-1
Library of Congress Control Number 2002 141381

Printed in Singapore

Editor: Rachel Cooke
Designer: John Calvert
Series Consultant: Dr. André Singer
Specialist Consultants: St John Simpson
Maps by Swanston Graphics Ltd and Eugene Fleury

Contents

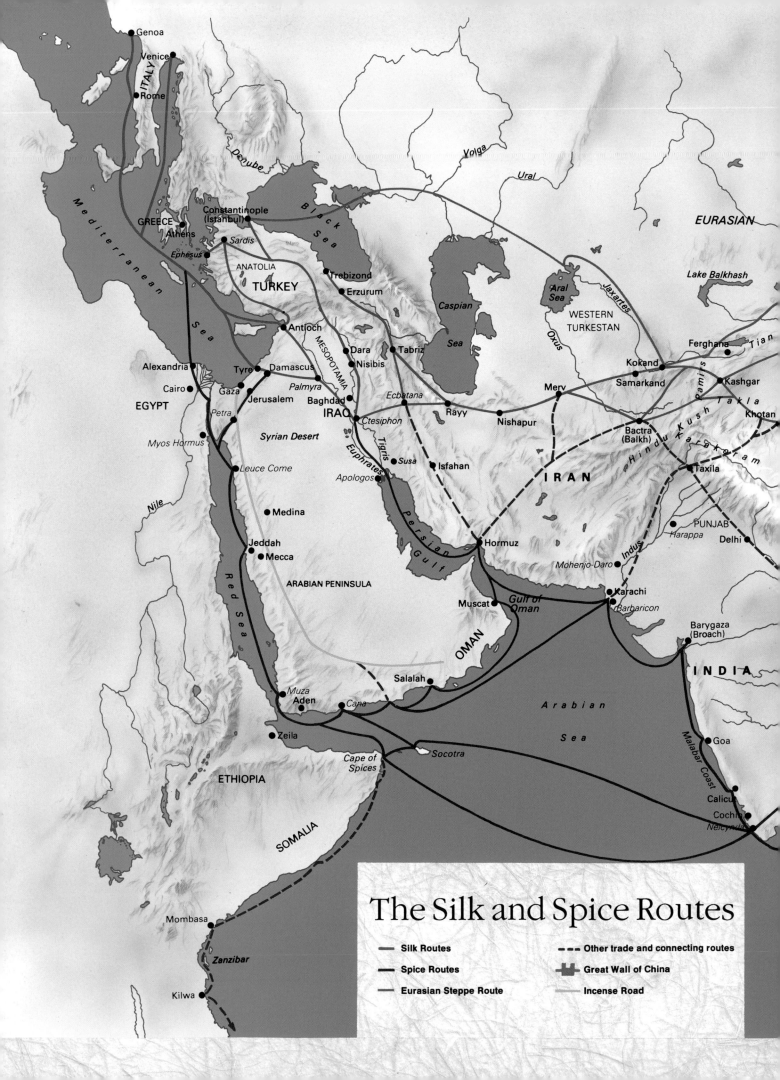

The Silk and Spice Routes

Legend:
- Silk Routes
- Spice Routes
- Eurasian Steppe Route
- Other trade and connecting routes
- Great Wall of China
- Incense Road

Genoa
Venice
Rome
ITALY
GREECE
Athens
Ephesus
Sardis
Constantinople (Istanbul)
ANATOLIA
TURKEY
Trebizond
Erzurum
Antioch
Mediterranean Sea
Alexandria
Cairo
EGYPT
Gaza
Tyre
Damascus
Jerusalem
Petra
Palmyra
Dara
Nisibis
Tabriz
MESOPOTAMIA
Baghdad
IRAQ
Ctesiphon
Ecbatana
Rayy
Susa
Isfahan
Apologos
Tigris
Euphrates
Syrian Desert
Nile
Myos Hormus
Leuce Come
Medina
Jeddah
Mecca
ARABIAN PENINSULA
Red Sea
Muza
Aden
Cana
Zeila
Cape of Spices
ETHIOPIA
SOMALIA
Mombasa
Zanzibar
Kilwa
Black Sea
Danube
Volga
Ural
Caspian Sea
Aral Sea
WESTERN TURKESTAN
Oxus
Jaxartes
EURASIAN
Lake Balkhash
Ferghana
Kokand
Samarkand
Kashgar
Merv
Nishapur
Bactra (Balkh)
Khotan
Takla
Tian
Pamirs
Hindu Kush
Karakoram
Taxila
PUNJAB
Harappa
Delhi
INDIA
Mohenjo-Daro
Indus
Karachi
Barbaricon
Barygaza (Broach)
Goa
Malabar Coast
Calicut
Cochin
Nelcynda
IRAN
Hormuz
Persian Gulf
Muscat
Gulf of Oman
OMAN
Salalah
Socotra
Arabian Sea

A Bridge between East and West

▲ *This partly-gilded silver plate from northern India shows an animal from Iranian myth. This type of metalwork was made by Sasanian craftsmen from Iran during the fourth and eighth centuries A.D. and even reached China via the Silk Route. The Chinese often copied Sasanian motifs in their own art and clothing.*

▶ *Paths on the Silk Route would often be as broken and difficult to cross as this mountain pass in Iran.*

Did you know?

Although the Silk Route was in regular use for over 1,600 years, it was never known as the Silk Route during this period. In fact, it had no overall name at all. A hundred years ago, the German explorer Baron Ferdinand von Richtofen referred to it as *die Seidenstrasse,* which means "The Silk Route," — in German.

"There is snow both in winter and summer, winds, rain, drifting sand, and gravel stones. The road is difficult and broken, with steep crags and precipices in the way. The mountainside is simply a stone wall standing up 10,000 feet . . . on going forward, there is no sure foothold." This passage is taken from the writings of the fifth-century Chinese pilgrim, Fa Xian. It describes some of the terrifying conditions he met as he traveled along stretches of the Silk Route on his pilgrimage to India from China.

This ancient route linked China in the East with Europe in the West, crossing through the heart of the Asian landmass. Its interlocking paths covered a distance of over 4,960 miles! Many different people lived along the Silk Route's paths. These included not only the Chinese and the Europeans, but the many peoples of central Asia and the Middle East Huns, Mongols, Iranians, Arabs, and Turks to name but a few. During the 1600 years of its existence, the Silk Route acted as a channel of communication between these diverse cultures.

But why did the extraordinary route come about? The simplest answer is trade, the buying and selling of goods. Since earliest times, people have traded goods with their neighbors. Certain prized goods were passed on from one tribe to the next, causing distinct trading routes to emerge. Gradually, these routes joined together to extend over huge distances. Each separate tribe of community was like a link in a chain and the trade brought wealth and prestige to each link.

It was around the start of the first century before the birth of Christ that the many different links in a long trading chain came together to form what we now call the Silk Route. For the first time, European gold could buy the luxuries of China, including the silk that gives the route its name. But it was a difficult exchange. As Fa Xian describes, the route crossed some dangerous terrain and the traders also faced the possibility of attack from marauding tribesmen and bandits. The Silk Route was safest and most successful when its paths were protected by powerful empires. Thus the history of these empires, their rise and fall, directly affected the fortunes of the Silk Route, from its early origins until its final decline around A.D. 1500, when sea routes took over as the main trade links between East and West.

▲ *The Silk Route had to cross one of two high mountain ranges in central Asia, the Karakorams or the Pamirs. This peak in the Karakorams is over 25,584 ft high.*

In its turn, the Silk Route had a deep effect on history. Before its coming, the Chinese and the Europeans had no idea of each other's existence! Along the paths of the Silk Route traveled not only goods but knowledge of different lands and people, as well as their cultures and beliefs. It is this knowledge that has been the Silk Route's greatest influence on history and its most lasting legacy for us today.

▲ *A trading caravan of merchants and camels. This detail is taken from a 14th-century map called* The Golden Road to Samarkand. *It was based on information brought back to Europe by Marco Polo, the most famous of the Silk Route explorers.*

To the Roof of the World

▲ The Silk Route was not just used by trading caravans but traveling pilgrims such as Buddhist monks and friars. This picture shows one such friar. It is part of a ninth-century mural from Dunhuang on the Silk Route, where a famous Buddhist shrine grew up.

▼ The fertile strip if the Gansu Corridor is hemmed in on two sides by barren mountains.

The eastern starting point of the Silk Route was Changan (modern-day Xi'an), the ancient capital of the Chinese Empire. From there, the traders and their caravans of camels set out west along the Gansu Corridor, a strip of fertile land which stretched over 496 miles to Dunhuang. This city was at the western end of the Great Wall of China, which the Chinese had built to protect themselves from the war-like tribes to the north. For the ancient Chinese, Dunhuang was considered the edge of the civilized world.

The next stage of the Silk Road crossed one of the most inhospitable stretches of terrain on the surface of the globe: the Tarim Basin. This vast natural basin today forms part of the northeastern Chinese province known as Xinjiang. It is over 930 miles long and 465 miles wide and is surrounded on three sides by mountain ranges rising to over 19,680 ft. Its eastern end opens into the Gobi Desert. In the midst of the Tarim Basin lies the Taklamakan, a desert of high, shifting sand dunes that have buried entire cities over the centuries. Mongolian, Turkic, Iranian, and Chinese people inhabit this desolate region. They live in small, isolated cities on the edge of the Taklamakan at the foot of the surrounding mountains. The patches of fertile ground around these cities are watered by the spring torrents from the melting glaciers of the peaks beyond.

◀ *Brightly-colored silks are still sold today in the market place at Kashgar, just as they were over 2,000 years ago.*

Travelers on the Silk Road could choose to skirt north or south around the Taklamakan Desert, covering the long hazardous journey in a series of stages from oasis to oasis. This part of the journey was very hard. Temperatures could range from –4°F to over 104°F and swirling sandstorms were a constant hazard.

From the southern path, it was possible to cross over the Karakoram Mountains into India, but the main north and south trails met up again at Kashgar, which marked the half-way point of the Silk Route. Still a thriving community today, this city lies at the foot of the Pamir Mountains. These had peaks which rise to over 24,600 ft. Their height and central position on the globe have led them to be called "The Roof of the World."

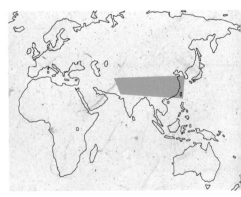

▶ *Map of the main paths of the Silk Route from Changan to Kashgar.*

The Silk Route caravans now had to cross one of the high passes over the Pamirs to continue their journey to the West. Here, the trail often consisted of little more than narrow rock ledges 14,760 ft up along the sides of sheer cliffs. The caravaners, with their precious cargoes of silk, were forced to battle their way through snowstorms and faced the danger of avalanches and falling rocks. It must have been only the thought of the vast profit at the end of their journey that kept them going.

The Route to Europe

After crossing the snowy passes of the Pamir Mountains, the trails of the Silk Route descended through a series of narrow valleys to the plains of Western Turkestan. Today, this area lies in northern Afghanistan and in Uzbekistan and Turkmenistan, south of the Aral Sea. Here, the Silk Route passed into a pleasant land of green fields, gardens, and orchards watered by two great rivers: the Oxus (now known as Amudar'ya) and the Jaxartes (or Syrdar'ya).

▶ *Map of the main paths of the Silk Route from the Pamirs to the Mediterranean.*

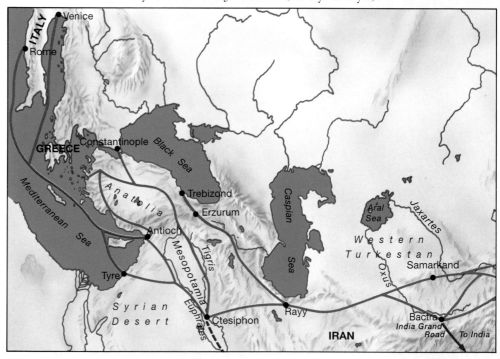

▼ *The Silk Route passed through the rich pastures of the Anatolian Plateau in central Turkey on its way to the Black Sea and Turkey.*

The Silk Route continued to follow several trails at this point. Many of the caravans would trade in goods from India and so continued down the southern trail to Bactra (later called Balkh). For centuries, the Indian Great Road (the trading route up from the Punjab plain) ended here. This meeting of two great trading routes made Bactra into an important trading center. In its bazaars and markets, goods from as far afield as China, Malaysia, the Middle East, and Europe were exchanged. For a time, the trade enabled Bactra to become one of the world's great cities — an equal of Rome, Baghdad, and Changan. But as the sea routes to India gained in importance, so overland trade dwindled and with it the wealth that made Bactra great.

The main northern trail of the Silk Route passed through Samarkand (now in Uzbekistan, part of the former Soviet Union) and then continued up on to the Iranian plateau to Rayy (which is just outside modern-day Tehran, the capital of Iran). From here, the Silk Route divided again. One route turned north to Trebizond on the Black Sea while the other descended into the fertile land of Mesopotamia, watered by the Tigris and Euphrates rivers. During the centuries the Silk Route passed through this region, many great empires rose and fell. Among these were the Parthian and Sasanian empires of Iran and the Muslim caliphates. Each of these empires came to rely on the wealth created by the Silk Route trade.

After Mesopotamia, the Silk Route continued northwest skirting the Syrian Desert before splitting once more into several trails. Some routes headed north across Anatolia (in modern Turkey) to Constantinople (now Istanbul), capital of the eastern Roman Empire from A.D. 330. Other trails fanned out to ports such as Tyre and Antioch, on the eastern shores of the Mediterranean. In these ports, silk and other valuable oriental merchandise was sold for gold and transported by ship to Rome — or, in later times, to whatever great European cities had wealth to squander on the luxuries of the East.

▲ *Funerary bust of a rich man from Palmyra carved between* A.D. *50–150. Palmyra was a Roman city in the Middle East made wealthy by trade with the East.*

◀ *Many castles, such as this one in eastern Turkey, were built along the Silk Routes. Most gave protection to the trade caravans, but some were home to the bandits who made a living by attacking and stealing from the traders.*

The Many Roads of the Silk Route

▲ *The ruins of Sardis in Turkey. This ancient city was the starting point for Darius' Persian Royal Road.*

As we have seen, the Silk Route consisted of more than just one single road linking East and West. At certain points it divided into a number of side routes. It split to avoid the hazards of the Taklamakan Desert. It crossed the Pamir Mountains by a number of different passes and followed several distinct routes across Western Turkestan. And at the western end it forked into different routes: to the eastern Mediterranean shore, overland through Anatolia (in modern Turkey), and up to the shores of the Black Sea. These alternative routes would wax and wane in importance depending upon which was safest, or who held power in the regions they crossed.

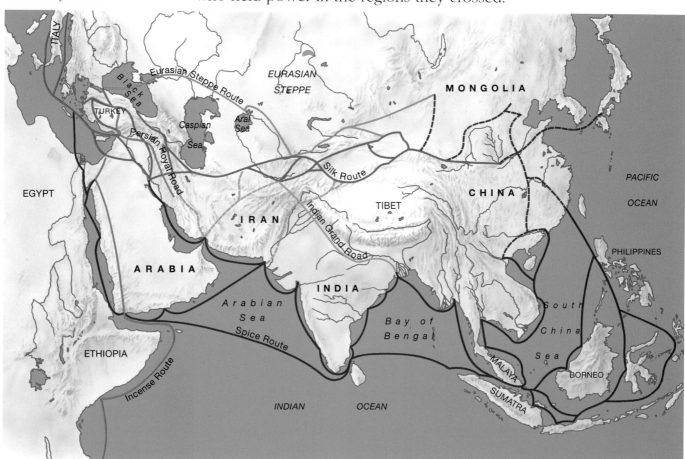

▲ *Map outlining the many trade routes that linked East and West.*

The overall title "The Silk Route" also includes such important tributaries as the Eurasian Steppe Route. This route crossed central Asia through the vast Steppe lands to the north of the Tian Shan Mountains, which lie on the northern edge of the Tarim Basin. Joining the main route briefly in Western Turkestan, it then headed northwest

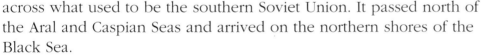

▲ Colorful spices, such as these, formed a major part of the trade across Asia and gave their name to the sea routes.

◄ A covered bazaar in Afghanistan. Money and goods would change hands many times in bazaars and markets such as this, linked across Asia by the trade routes.

across what used to be the southern Soviet Union. It passed north of the Aral and Caspian Seas and arrived on the northern shores of the Black Sea.

The Silk Route incorporated part of an even older overland route, the Persian Royal Road. This was established at the turn of the fifth century B.C. by the Persian Emperor Darius. This road traveled over a thousand miles between Darius' capital Susa in Persia and Anatolia, and Darius encouraged trade to pass along it. In 331 B.C., the route found a different use as Alexander the Great and his Greek army traveled over stretches of it on their long march of conquest.

The Silk Route also linked up with several other great trading routes. The Indian Grand Road brought spices up from the Punjab over the Hindu Kush to join the Silk Route at Bactra. The Incense Road, carrying oriental perfumes, led up from the southern shore of Arabia to join the Silk Route at Damascus. Here in the Syrian heartland, the Silk Route was also joined by a branch of the Spice Route. This was largely a sea route, which led down the Red Sea, across the Indian Ocean to India, and beyond to the south coast of China. This was the Silk Route's main alternative in trade with the East. During the periods when the Silk Route was too dangerous for traders, silk would often come from China by ship along this much longer (but often much safer) route.

▲ This 13th-century flask, made in Afghanistan was sent to India, probably via the Indian Grand Road.

13

chapter two

The Opening of the Silk Route

Zhang Qian's Expedition

In the second century B.C., two great powers were beginning to emerge in the world. In the West, Rome was gaining control through Europe and the Near East. Meanwhile in the Far East, after a period of civil war, China became reunited under a series of great emperors. These emperors came from the Han family, and the period of their rule is known as the Han Dynasty. It was under the Han Dynasty that the Chinese Empire began to spread westward.

Yet despite China's newfound strength, north and west China were constantly threatened by raids from nomadic Mongol and Turkic tribes. In particular, there was a tribe the Chinese called the Xiongnu (later known in Europe as the Huns). In order to protect themselves from these raiders, the Chinese needed horses. At this period, the only horses the Chinese possessed were a small, pony-like breed, but they had begun to hear reports of a new kind of horse. This was large and strong, and capable of carrying armor-clad men into battle. According to the reports these "heavenly horses" (as the Chinese called them) were bred by the people who lived in the valleys of Ferghana. These valleys lay beyond China to the northwest, on the other side of the Tian Shan Mountains.

▲ *This beautiful bronze horse was made in China during the Han Dynasty. Its foot is balanced on a swallow enabling it to fly. The "heavenly horses" of Ferghana inspired the creation of many works of art during the Han Dynasty.*

The Han Emperor, Wu-di, decided to send an expedition to Ferghana to find these horses. The man he chose to lead this expedition was Zhang Qian. In 138 B.C., Zhang set off westward from the imperial capital of Changan on what was to become one of history's greatest trips of exploration. Together with his expedition of 100 men, he journeyed to the western end of the Great Wall of China, which had been built to protect the Chinese Empire from the northern barbarians. From there he ventured forth towards the notorious Taklamakan desert, which he was told meant in local dialect: "Go into this place and you won't come out alive."

▲ *The Tian Shan or "Heavenly" Mountains. Zhang Qian had to cross the western end of this high range to reach Ferghana.*

◀ *The Silk Route crossed this barren landscape in the Tarim Basin. It has changed very little since Zhang Qian passed through this remote area on his long journey.*

Zhang found a way around this death-trap by traveling between the remote oases which skirted the desert. Next he had to deal with the high passes over the Tian Shan Mountains to Ferghana. All this time, Zhang was in danger from the Xiongnu. Twice he was taken prisoner and one of these periods of captivity was to last for over ten years! Finally, after thirteen years of adventure and hard traveling, Zhang managed to make it back to Changan. He had only one companion left from his original expedition of 100 men.

The Emperor Wu-di had long given up hope for Zhang and his expedition, believing that they were all dead. Zhang told the amazed court that the stories they had heard about the "heavenly horses" of Ferghana were true. According to a Chinese historian of the period, Zhang also told of an empire he had heard of called Persia, and a fabulous empire to its southeast, India.

Zhang Qian was not the first to travel across the mountains to the West. This route had almost certainly been used by occasional traders for several centuries. But it was through Zhang Qian that China discovered the potential for trade with the West, thus laying the foundations for what was eventually to be known as the Silk Route.

▲ Acrobats and tumblers have been popular in China for a long time. Many trace the traditions of their art back to the Han Dynasty when entertainers from western Asia came to China by way of the Silk Route.

The Golden Age of the Han Dynasty

As a result of Zhang Qian's expedition, the Emperor Wu-di sent another mission to Ferghana. He wanted to buy some of the "heavenly horses" in order to defend China again the Xiongnu. But the people of Ferghana believed that their horses were sacred, and refused to sell them to the Chinese. So the Emperor Wu-di next despatched a huge army of 60,000 men over 1,488 miles across the mountains to capture some "heavenly horses."

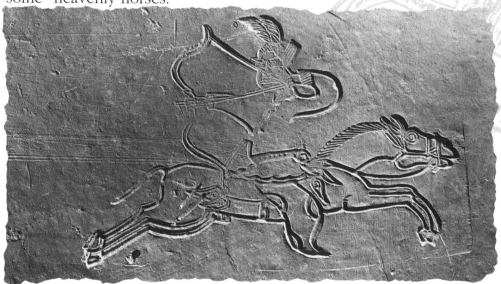

▶ A stone relief depicting a mounted Chinese warrior, dating from the Han Dynasty. The Chinese adopted the tactic of fighting on horseback from the Xiongnu.

▼ The green area on this map shows the extent of the Chinese Empire around A.D. 100.

It was a massive undertaking, but the Emperor Wu-di's expedition was a great success. It managed to capture a breeding herd of these new large horses, which was brought back to China. In the course of this successful campaign, the Xiongnu were driven from north-western China, and Chinese power spread across the entire Tarim Basin. Caravans could now safely journey through the region and traders soon began exploring this new route carrying bales of silk from China, bringing back precious jade from the mountains of the Tarim Basin.

But this was only the beginning. The traders discovered that silk was a highly valued commodity in the West and soon began exporting their wares beyond the Pamir Mountains. Under protection of the newly-expanded Chinese Empire, the caravans began opening up the Silk Route to the West.

The Han emperors encouraged this trade and, perhaps for the first time, the Chinese began to look at the world beyond their borders for reasons other than the need to defend themselves. The trading caravans returning from the West along the Silk Route arrived in China with all kinds of new wonders never before seen in the East, and bearing tales of the empires in the West. For the first time, the Chinese annals mentioned the empire of "Li-Gan" — a name that seems to refer to the Roman Empire.

Chinese silk was exchanged for luxuries such as furs, precious stones, and ivory. The traders introduced cucumbers, grapes, figs, and many other foods to China. The Chinese word for grape comes from the Greek. This is a clear indication that the fruit arrived in China from the West, probably via Bactria (part of present day Afghanistan) which was at that time a Greek speaking region famous for its vineyards.

The golden age of the Han Dynasty had begun. From around 100 B.C. China entered a period of great progress and stability that was to last for over a century. Historical records dating from the period give us some idea of how much of China's rapid progress during the Han Dynasty came as a result of trade with the West by way of the Silk Route.

▼ *This jade burial suit, held together by gold wire, was made for the Han Princess You Wan. Jade was highly prized by the Chinese and the newly-opened Silk Route gave them access to the rich deposits of this stone found around the Tarim Basin.*

Silk and the Roman Empire

▲ *The red area on this map shows the extent of the Roman Empire around A.D. 100.*

While the Han Dynasty prospered in the East, the Roman Empire continued to grow in the West. By the birth of Christ, the Roman Empire stretched from northern France to the shores of North Africa, and from Spain in the west to the eastern shores of the Mediterranean. This guaranteed protection for trading caravans at the western end of the Silk Route.

As capital of this empire, Rome became a city of great wealth and sophistication importing products from far and wide. When Chinese silk first reached Rome, it caused a sensation. The Romans had never before seen such fine material, and silk garments became the height of fashion among the aristocracy. In no time, silk was in great demand, and its popularity began to spread throughout the Roman Empire. The Romans could not get enough silk to satisfy the demand, and silk began to fetch huge prices. It was literally worth its weight in gold!

▼ *Roman women would have worn clothes like these, some of them made from highly-fashionable silk.*

◀ *These magnificent Roman ruins from Ephesus (in modern-day Turkey) give some idea of the wealth of the Roman Empire. Much of this wealth was spent on luxuries from the East.*

▼ *Silken twine being put onto reels by hand. Today, this is usually done by machines.*

▼ *Silk worms spinning their cocoons in a bamboo tray.*

Making Silk

The silkworm is the caterpillar of a large flightless moth simply known as the silk moth. When changing from caterpillar to moth, the silkworm spins a cocoon around itself for protection. The inner part of the this cocoon is a continuous strand of very fine silk that can measure up to 2,952 ft in length. Silk farmers unravel this strand and entwine it with as many as fourteen others to produce the silken thread. This can then be woven into silk cloth.

The craze for silk and other eastern luxuries led to huge amounts of Roman money and gold being sent eastward to trading centers across Asia, from the Middle East to India and beyond. Early in the first century A.D., the emperor Tiberius complained that the riches of the empire were being drained away by what he saw as needless extravagance: "In exchange for trifles, our money is sent to foreign lands and even to our enemies." But the silk continued to be bought.

The Roman historian Pliny refers to a form of silk being produced on the Greek island of Cos — but the art of sericulture, silk making, was largely unknown in the West. Under the Han Dynasty, the Chinese were careful to keep knowledge of this art secret, so that they could continue to make huge profits from the silk which was shipped west along the Silk and Spice Routes.

▲ *Map of the four empires crossed by the Silk Route around A.D.100: the Roman (red area), the Parthian (blue area), the Kushtan (orange area), and the Chinese (green area).*

The Middle Empires

For much of the first two centuries after Christ, traders along the eastern end of the Silk Route were protected by the Chinese Empire. Similarly, at the western end of the Silk Route, traders were guaranteed safe passage by the Roman Empire. But there still remained the lands between these two empires. During the Roman-Han period, this region was largely controlled by two peoples, the Parthians and the Kushans.

An Iranian tribe from southeast of the Caspian Sea, the Parthians had a well-established empire stretching from the Pamirs to the Syrian desert by the start of the first century B.C. The newly-opened Silk

Route passed through this territory, and the Parthians soon began to prosper as middlemen. They would levy taxes on the caravans passing through their territory, in exchange for protection. Also, their traders would buy goods from the incoming caravans and re-sell them at a profit to other caravans passing through their territory.

▲ *A group of Parthian warriors carved in stone relief. Note their pants, which show that they were horsemen.*

In the first century A.D. the Parthians began to lose control of the eastern end of their empire. This allowed the Kushans, a tribe from northern China, to establish a large empire in central Asia. They, too, saw the benefits of trade and encouraged it by protecting the routes through the Pamirs and the trading centers of Samarkand and Bactra

Relationships between the Chinese and the Kushans were relatively good, but the Romans and Parthians were not on such friendly terms. Rome resented paying huge prices for goods that had passed through Parthian lands and, in an attempt to bypass the middleman, looked more to the sea routes from the Red Sea to Indian as a means of obtaining Eastern goods. But so long as these four empires remained stable and able to protect the trade routes, overland trade flourished.

▼ *This Parthian pendant dates from the first century A.D. It is made of gold studded with garnets. Garnets and other colored stones were some of the most expensive items traded along the Silk Route.*

◀ *This great arch is the world's largest unsupported brick vault. It is part of a palace in Ctesiphon, the capital of the Parthian (and later Sasanian) Empire and a wealthy center for Silk Route trade.*

▲ *A view of modern-day Istanbul, formerly Constantinople. The Roman Emperor Constantine gave the city his name when he made it his capital in* A.D. *330.*

▶ *An 18th-century Chinese drawing of two Xiongnu warriors. The Xiongnu were a constant threat to Chinese control of the Tarim Basin throughout the period of the Han Dynasty.*

chapter three

Controlling the Silk Route

Collapse of the Old Empires

Vast empires such as Rome and Han China possessed are hard to maintain. Through the whole of the Roman-Han period, the stability that allowed the trade routes to prosper was constantly under threat and would occasionally break down altogether.

The Han Dynasty's official history records the exploits of a general called Ban Chao. In A.D. 73 he took an army into the Tarim Basin, where the constant raids of the Xiongnu (Huns) had dislodged Chinese power and upset Silk Route trade. It was a successful campaign and led to increased contact between China and the Kushan and Parthian Empires. But Rome and Han China were never to meet, perhaps because of sheer distance or perhaps through the intervention of the middle empires keen to maintain control of the lucrative East-West trade. During the third century A.D., the constant threats to Han China's stability finally became irresistible. Floods and famine resulted in a series of rebellions throughout the empire, seriously weakening the power of the Han. Warlords seized control of provincial cities and the Xiongnu once again attacked from the north. With the death of the last Hun Emperor in A.D. 220, the dynasty came to an end and China divided into a series of smaller, unstable kingdoms.

The Roman Empire was also beginning to crumble. The cost of Eastern luxuries and maintaining large armies had drained its economy, leaving it almost bankrupt. Recovery was hampered by internal revolts and the barbarian invasions from northern Europe and Asia. In A.D. 330, the Emperor Constantine selected Constantinople at the mouth of the Black Sea as his new capital, reflecting the gradual shift eastward of Roman interests. Over the next few centuries, the empire was to lose control of its Western European and North African territories. The remaining lands became known as the Byzantine Empire (taking its name from Constantinople's old name, Byzantium).

▲ *The marble head of the Roman Emperor Constantine who ruled from A.D. 306 to 363. This was part of a colossal sculpture that stood over 49 ft high.*

◄ *An excavation of a Silk Route town on the southern edge of the Taklamakan conducted by Sir Aurel Stein in 1901. The wooden carvings on the site date from around A.D. 200 and reveal how the inhabitants were much influenced by styles from northern India and Iran. Stein also found evidence that the settlement was abandoned about A.D. 270. He concluded that this was probably a result of the breakdown of Chinese power in the Tarim. Basin which followed the end of the Han Dynasty.*

The Romans' old adversaries, the Parthians, had also been having problems maintaining their empire. In A.D. 224, they were finally ousted by a powerful and militaristic tribe from southern Iran called the Sasanians. Not content with the lands of Mesopotamia and Iran, the Sasanians swept down the Indian Grand Road to take on the Kushans. From the middle of the third century A.D., they completely dominated the Silk Route territories between the Pamirs and the Euphrates.

During all this upheaval, overland trade inevitably declined — but it did not cease altogether. The Byzantines still bought silk in large quantities and the Chinese, despite their internal problems, still contrived to send the material eastward to meet this demand by land, and increasingly by sea. The Sasanians, like the Parthians before them, swiftly took on the profitable role of middlemen.

Sasanians and Sogdians

▲ *A Sasanian glass bottle dating from fifth to sixth centuries A.D. Sasanian glass such as this has been found as far east as Japan.*

▼ *A present day Kyrgyz caravan of Bactrian camels passing through the Pamirs, just as the Sogdian caravans did centuries before.*

The Silk and Spice Routes flourished under the Sasanians. Their government maintained a rigid control of the trade and imposed heavy taxes on all goods passing between their land and the Byzantine Empire. This was made possible by the network of forts that lined the Sasanian-Byzantine borders. The only official route that was open to trade passed between the heavily-fortified border cities of Nisibis and Dara. It is still possible to trace this part of the Silk Route in northern Mesopotamia as frequent traffic has left a heavily-worn track crossing the landscape.

Further east, the Sasanians shared the role of middlemen with the Sogdians. A tribe from the Samarkand region, the Sogdians had first risen to prominence on the Silk Route under the Kushans. They took caravans over the Pamirs and around the Tarim Basin, sometimes as far as Dunhuang. Alongside the Sasanians, the Sogdians developed their reputation as the merchants of central Asia. They established several communities along the northern edge of the Tarim Basin, and this was helped by their knowledge of sophisticated irrigation techniques.

No longer protected by the Han, the techniques of sericulture and silk weaving had slowly spread westward, although China continued to produce the best quality silken twine and material. Using Chinese thread Sasanian and Sogdian silk-weaving industries flourished from central Asia to Mesopotamia. Few examples of these silks still survive, but some made their way to Europe where they have been found wrapped around sacred relics. Other fragments have been discovered at Buddhist cave sites in the Tarim Basin. Their motifs and style have heavily influenced the later designs of Chinese, Byzantine, and Muslim cloth.

▲ *This Sasanian gold plate with silver relief shows the fourth-century King Shapur II out hunting.*

Sasanian and Sogdian decorated metal bowls and jugs were also highly prized. Other vessels made from thick clear glass with elaborate cut decoration are typical Sasanian products. These were traded as far as Japan where they were used by the imperial family. Objects like these provide definite evidence that the Silk Route was still functioning.

It is very unlikely that any merchants took part in direct, long-distance trade. Instead, the exact size and composition of a given caravan must have changed with every stop and supply of fresh pack animals. In addition, one-humped camels (dromedaries or cross-breeds) and mules were used for the western parts of the Silk Route, whereas only the shaggy haired, two-humped Bactrian camels were capable of crossing the cold and hot extremes of the Pamir mountains and the Taklamakan desert.

▲ *Two Sasanian iron swords, one with a finely worked gold scabbard, both dating from the sixth to seventh centuries A.D.*

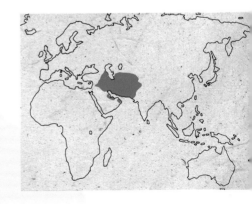

▲ *A map of the Sasanian Empire in A.D. 531 when it was at its greatest extent.*

Buddhism

The Buddhist religion originated in India in the sixth century B.C. However, it was not until the first century A.D., with the trade routes fully open, that the religion spread up through Kushan and Sogdian territory into the Tarim Basin, and later into China itself. Archeologists have uncovered many Buddhist statues and religious tracts throughout these areas. Indeed, Buddhist monasteries with their characteristic stupas are found in most ancient central Asian cities. This silk badge (below) showing the Buddha with an alms bowl dates from seventh to eigth centuries A.D. It was found at the Buddhist cave shrines at Dunhuang.

Zoroastrianism

Zoroastrianism is named after the prophet Zoroaster. He probably lived during the seventh century B.C., but the religion's origin may be earlier than this. During the third to sixth centuries A.D., it flourished as the official religion of the Sasanian Empire. Zoroastrians worship fire as a symbol of their god and many ruined "fire temples" are found in Iran. Similarly, Zoroastrian artifacts found in central Asia dating from this time show that the religion had spread beyond Iran. Zoroastrianism is still practiced today, particularly among the Parsi community in India who came there from Iran to trade around 900 A.D.

chapter four

The Paths of New Beliefs

The Spread of Religions

The merchants who traveled the Silk Route did not just carry goods with them, but also brought ideas. In particular, the Silk Routes were a major channel for the spread of religions throughout Asia and Europe. The first thousand years after Christ brought huge changes in religious thinking. Older religions such as Buddhism spread from India into central Asia and China, while several new religions emerged — including Christianity and Islam. Each religion was to exercise a huge influence on its followers, not just in their everyday life but also in their arts, literature, and politics. These religious influences are reflected in the archeological finds made along the Silk Route.

Byzantine Christian churches were often decorated with beautiful mosaics such as this one. It depicts a scene from the Bible, but the characters are dressed in clothes from the Byzantine period.

A 15th-century copy of the Qur'an.

Three bronze Nestorian crosses, found in China and dating from the 11–14th centuries.

A fifth-century Sasanian bronze figurine of Ahriman, the Zoroastrian God of Evil.

A modern Zoroastrian fire temple in Iran.

Islam

Islam was founded in Arabia by the Prophet Muhammad in A.D 622, following his flight from the city of Mecca to Medina. It was the last of the world religions to pass along the Silk Route and is still practiced along many of its paths. The religion spread rapidly through the Middle East and North Africa to reach Spain, central Asia, and India by 750 A.D.

The picture here is a copy of the Qur'an, the Muslim's sacred text. The Qur'an is always written in Arabic and often decorated with beautiful, intricate patterns. This style of decoration has developed because Muslim law traditionally forbids the portrayal of living figures.

Christianity

From the death of Jesus around A.D. 30, Christianity spread through parts of the Near East and Europe, despite persecution. In the fourth century it was adopted by the Roman ruling classes and gradually became more organized with a set of recognized beliefs. However, some groups or sects held to slightly different beliefs. One such sect was the Nestorians (named after a theologian called Nestorious). They were allowed to establish themselves in the Sasanian Empire after they fled Byzantine persecution in the fifth-century. Nestorian crosses (such as in the picture) are commonly found in central Asia and China, in the form of pendants or on tombstones.

The Pilgrim Explorers

▼ *This Buddhist cave complex at Bamiyan was visited by Xuan-Zang on his pilgrimage. The statue of the Buddha carved into the rock here was over 114 ft high. It was destroyed in 2001.*

Although Buddhist pilgrims probably began reaching China in the first or second century A.D., this new Indian religion was not at first accepted by the Chinese. Not until the last troubled years of the Han Dynasty did the Chinese begin turning to Buddhism in large numbers.

During the unstable period which followed the Han Dynasty, China was largely cut off from India. The Chinese became worried that in isolation they might have strayed from the "true path" of the Buddhists in India. In A.D. 399 they sent a pilgrim called Fa Xian to India to find out if this was the case. Fa Xian's record of his daring journey along the unprotected Silk Route to India is one of the few descriptions we have of the eastern end of the Silk Route during this period. According to Fa Xian, crossing the Taklamakan was sometimes so dangerous that "it was impossible to know the way but for dead men's decaying bones, which showed the direction." When Fa Xian eventually arrived in India, he was an object of great wonder. This was the first time the Indians had seen a man from "the Land of Han" (as they called China). It was to be twelve years before Fa Xian finally made it back to China, by way of the Spice Route.

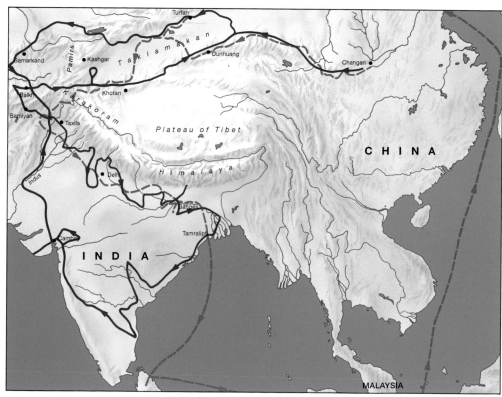

▶ *A map showing the routes covered by Fa Xian and Xuan-Zang on their journeys from China to India and back. Fa Xian's route is shown by the broken line, Xuan-Zang's by the solid one.*

◀ *A modern Buddhist monk in Nepal carrying a prayer wheel. Behind him is a sacred stupa inset with prayer wheels.*

▼ *A seventh-century wall hanging from Dunhuang depicting a Chinese pilgrim laden with manuscripts and sutras. It may well be a representation of Xuan-Zang on his return to China.*

Two centuries later, the Buddhists realized that many of their sacred books had been mistranslated from the original Indian texts. This led to serious errors in Buddhist practice. So another pilgrim, a learned man called Xuan-Zang, decided to set out along the Silk Route for India to seek out the original Indian Buddhist holy books. Xuan-Zang was to survive many adventures on his travels, including a murder attempt! Traveling via Samarkand and Bactria, his record of the journey provides us with first-hand details of the people he met. For example, he describes how half the Sogdians lived by agriculture, the other half by trade.

But when Xuan-Zang finally arrived in India, he found "a thousand monasteries lay deserted in ruins, overgrown with weeds," many destroyed by the invasions of the Huns during the fifth Century A.D.. In northern and central India, people had forsaken Buddhism and returned to the Hindu religion.

Xuan-Zang wandered throughout Indian for nearly sixteen years. He visited Buddhist holy places and found the religion thrived in the east of the country. He collected Indian holy books to take back with him to China.

On Xuan-Zang's return to China, the new Emperor Taizong was so impressed with his exploits that he offered Xuan-Zang a post as his imperial adviser. But Xuan-Zang chose to retire to a monastery and complete his task, making a faithful translation of the sacred Buddhist books he had brought back from India.

The Tang Dynasty

The Emperor Taizong, who welcomed Xuan-Zang on his return from India, was the first emperor of the Tang Dynasty. United under his new royal family, China was once more entering a great age. Trade boomed and major innovations were made both in technology and the arts. All this took place while much of Europe was plunged into the relative chaos that followed the decline of Roman power.

The Tang Emperors once again extended China's power into the Tarim Basin. Silk Route trade increased and the Chinese, perhaps more than ever before, welcomed the foreign influences that came with it. Nestorian Christians appeared at the imperial court. Sanskrit texts on medicine, mathematics, and astrology were imported from India. Motifs from Sasanian and Sogdian cloth and other wares were copied and embellished. Changan, at the eastern end of the Silk Route, once again became a great imperial capital. Its population expanded to over two million, with separate quarters for foreign traders who came to China in large numbers for the first time. The imperial annals record that in A.D. 643, the emperor received an ambassador from Fu-Lin, the Chinese name for Byzantium. This appears to have been an isolated incident though, for there is no other mention of direct contact between the Chinese and the Byzantine Empires.

▲ *This glazed figurine of a wine merchant from central Asia is one of the many found in the graves of Tang China. Tang pottery was often glazed in this three-colored style.*

▶ *A portrait of the Tang Emperor Tsong, who ruled China from A.D. 712–756.*

The Silk Route itself expanded, with caravans continuing beyond Changan as far as Korea and to the coast for shipment to Japan. The Tang records provide some of the most detailed descriptions of Silk Route trade. There are descriptions of exotic birds and animals — such as peacocks, parrots, and ostriches — as well as different medicines, aromatics, spices, fragrant woods, and precious stones. Rich Tang Dynasty tombs often contained large numbers of decorated clay figures of men and animals, often associated with trade. There are striking representatives of prancing horses — recalling the "heavenly horses" of Ferghana — and camels heavily laden with sacks or rolls of cloth.

At this time, major changes were also taking place at the western end of the Silk Route. A series of devastating Byzantine-Sasanian wars raged from southern Arabia (modern Yemen) across the Egypt, Syria, and the Black Sea — and shortly after this the two great empires crumbled in the seventh century A.D. In their place rose new kingdoms sharing a new official religion — Islam.

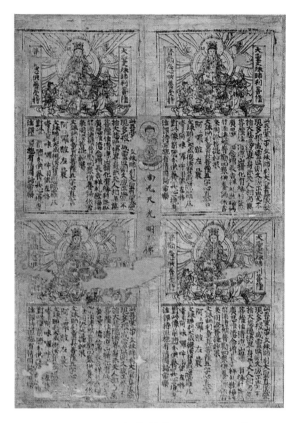

▲ *A 10th-century wooden block print of a sacred Buddhist text. Printing techniques were developed in Tang China during the ninth century — 600 years before the printing press was invented in Europe.*

▼ *The ruins of an ancient oasis city near Turfan. During the Tang Dynasty, a permanent garrison was stationed here to protect Silk Route travelers.*

The Rise of Islam

▲ *The extent of Muslim power (blue), the Byzantine Empire (red), and the Tang Empire (green) in A.D. 814.*

▶ *The interior of the Blue Mosque in Istanbul. The intricate designs on the walls and window were developed by Muslim artists who were forbidden to represent the human figure.*

▼ *The bottom dish is a typical example of Tang pottery. Their use of colored glazes was later imitated in the Middle East and Europe, resulting in dishes such as the upper two shown here.*

The Prophet Muhammad died in A.D. 632, leaving behind him an organized community of the new religion, Islam, through central and southern Arabia. From here, inspired by their religious fervour, the Muslim Arab armies began to push outward. They quickly overran much of the Byzantine and Sasanian empires, which were weakened by decades of war, plague, and economic neglect. By the year A.D. 670 — less than forty years after the death of Muhammad — the Arab armies had reached the river Oxus, although it took them several years to subdue this region. Control of the Silk Route from the Mediterranean to the Pamirs now passed into the hands of the Arabs and subsequent Islamic dynasties.

Soldiers, administrators, farmers, and craftsmen who had previously been Christians or Zoroastrians began to convert to Islam. This was at first a gradual process and the Middle East is still full of diverse peoples and religious sects. However, Islam was soon the dominant religion of Western Asia.

In A.D. 751, the Islamic army defeated a Chinese force in the Battle of Talas, east of Samarkand. Large numbers of Chinese craftsmen were taken prisoner, among whom were former silk workers and papermakers. These papermakers began to practice their craft again in Samarkand and knowledge of their techniques spread westward from there, reaching Baghdad by A.D. 794.

After its defeat at Talas, the Tang Empire began the troubled days of its long decline. Arab forces captured Kashgar and the Tarim Basin was overrun by the Tibetans from the south. The irrigation systems essential for settled life fell into decay and trade along this section of the Silk Route began to dwindle once again.

Maritime trade increased in importance as the Arabs were excellent seafarers. From the eighth century onward, they were sailing all the way to East Africa and China. Distinctive types of Chinese and Southeast Asian pottery began to appear in the Middle East from this period, and these were often copied by local craftsmen.

The tenth to thirteenth centuries marked a flowering of the Islamic civilization in the Middle East and central Asia, as East-West trade brought great wealth to the region. Magnificent mosques, tombs, and palaces were built — sometimes covered in colorful glazed tiles and painted inside with beautiful patterns and designs.

▼ *A 19th-century painting of an Arab market, a scene almost unchanged for centuries. Silk Route travelers in the Middle East would have encountered many such markets.*

▲ *A Kyrgyz tribesman of the Eurasian Steppe region, with his hunting eagle.*

chapter five

The Silk Route of the Mongols

The Coming of Ghengis Khan

At the end of the twelfth century, in the wastes of the Mongolian steppes to the north of China, events were taking place which were to change dramatically the course of history. The nomadic tribesmen, who had produced such fearsome warriors as the Huns (Xiongnu) were coming together under a great Mongolian leader. His name was Ghengis Khan.

Ghengis Khan was proclaimed leader of the Mongols at Karakorum (near Ulan Bator, the capital of modern Mongolia) in 1196. At the time, China was split in two. The south was ruled by the Sung Dynasty, and the north was already under a Manchurian Dynasty of Mongol origin. In the west, the Muslims were divided into a number of regional powers. There was no longer a great empire to confront the growing Mongol domination which now extended from eastern China to western Turkestan. Even so, no one foresaw the explosion of Mongol power which now took place.

▲ *Horse games such as this one are often played among the nomadic tribes of central and north-east Asia, echoing the horseback battles of their past.*

Ghengis Khan and his powerful army of Mongol horsemen spilled out of the eastern steppe and overran the surrounding territory in all directions. This was one of the most ferocious campaigns the world has ever known. Beijing, the new capital of northern China, was sacked — and its population either fled or was massacred on the spot. When offered resistance, the Mongol armies took no prisoners.

The Mongols then turned west beyond the Pamirs and attacked the Silk Route city of Merv. They are said to have massacred its 700,000 inhabitants — and even killed all the cats and dogs. Usually, however, the Mongols were careful to spare able-bodied men and craftsmen, who were systematically deported and re-employed elsewhere.

Soon, the Mongol Empire stretched all over China and into Afghanistan, through much of the Middle East and into Europe as far as Poland. Fast, safe lanes of communication were essential in order to control such a huge empire. One of these was the Silk Route, and overland trade was to prosper again under Mongol protection. A massive construction program of state caravanserais (multi-purpose roadside inns), post-houses, and bridges was implemented by the Mongols. Cities which they had previously destroyed, such as Samarkand, were to rise again.

For the first and last time in its long history, almost the entire length of the Silk Route was ruled by one power. Under what has become known as the *Pax Mongolica*, there was relative peace along its paths. The final great century of the Silk Route had begun.

▼ *A 14th-century Iranian manuscript illustration showing Ghengis Khan fighting the Chinese in the mountains.*

35

The Pope's Emissary to the East

▲ *Ghengis Khan on his throne surrounded by his court. John Carpini would have seen similar scenes when he attended the great international gathering at Karakorum, which was the Mongol capital.*

Mongol aggression was frequently held in check by the death of one of their leaders. Mongol armies poised to push out the boundaries of their empire still further would have to return to Mongolia for the election of a new ruler. In 1241, the death of Ogedei (Ghengis Khan's son, who had succeeded him) caused one such halt. Emissaries from all over the known world now traveled to the Mongol capital of Karakorum for the selection of a new leader. This was one of the greatest international meetings of its time, with representatives traveling from as far afield as Turkey and Korea, Russia and Rome.

Western Europe had by now emerged from the so-called Dark Ages to the more stable and prosperous Medieval period. Cities such as Venice and Genoa had built up trading links across the Mediterranean and were looking to extend their influence further eastward. It was perhaps with this in mind that the newly-elected Pope Innocent IV felt it necessary to send an emissary from Rome. More importantly, he had hopes of forming an alliance with the heathen Mongols and converting them to Christianity so protecting Europe from further Mongol expansion. The Pope chose as his emissary to Karakorum a friar called John Carpini.

Friar John Carpini traveled to Mongolia by way of the Eurasian Steppe Route, the branch of the Silk Route that crossed from the Black Sea north of the Caspian and skirted the Tarim Basin by a side route which kept north of the Tian Shan Mountains. In fact, this was geographically a much less hazardous and shorter route than the main Silk Route, but it had previously been vulnerable to raids from the war-like tribes who inhabited the Steppes through which it passed.

The tribes had now been defeated by the Mongols, making the route safe for caravans. During *Pax Mongolica*, the Eurasian Steppe Route was probably more popular than the main southern route. The Mongols even established what are known as the Golden Horde cities along the European end of its path, which they filled with craftsmen and other people transplanted from conquered lands.

But Friar John Carpini's mission to the Mongolian capital was not a success. Unlike the emissaries from all over the Empire, he had brought with him no lavish gifts for the new Khan. This was not appreciated. When the new Khan was selected, all the emissaries prostrated themselves before him except Friar John Carpini, who said he prostrated himself only before God. The Khan was not impressed by this obstinate Christian behavior. The Pope's hopes of forming an allegiance with the Mongols, and perhaps even converting them to Christianity, were dashed.

But despite his lack of tact, Friar John Carpini was an astute observer. When he returned to Rome, he told the Pope that he had noted signs of division amongst the Mongols. In his view, this could well divert the Mongols from further expansion into Western Europe. As it turned out, Friar John Carpini was right. From now on internal power struggles effectively halted any further Mongol expansion into Europe.

▼ *The interior of a yurt, the traditional tent dwelling of the nomadic tribes of Mongolia and central Asia.*

A yurt on the Mongolian Steppe today. As nomads, the Mongols seldom stayed in one place for any length of time and the easily-transported yurt was ideal for this lifestyle.

Marco Polo's Journey

▲ *A 13th-century figurine of a Chinese character actor, such as might have been found at Kublai Khan's court.*

▲ *A map showing the route covered by Marco Polo on his journey to and from China. The shaded area indicated the extent of the Mongol Empire at the time.*

With much of Asia now under Mongol rule and European trade expanding, it was now that the most famous of all European travelers to the East made his journey along the Silk Route. In 1271, Marco Polo set off from Venice for China, accompanied by his father and his uncle.

The two elder Polos had already traveled to China by way of the Eurasian Steppe Route in search of trade. They had been well received by the Mongol ruler Kublai Khan, who had never before seen any "Latins." The elder Polos had been quick to see the possibilities of trade with the East and promised Kublai Khan they would return.

Marco Polo has left us with a detailed description of his 5,580-mile journey to China, filled with many adventures. He passed along the Silk Route from Turkey, down through the Persian Gulf to Hormuz, north again to Balkh, across the Pamirs to Kashgar, and then took the southern route around the Tarim Basin into China itself. Even under the protection of the Mongol Empire, the Silk Route had its dangers. In remote regions of Iran, Marco Polo recorded that "unless merchants be well armed they run the risk of being murdered, or at least robbed of everything." Three years after setting out, the Polos finally arrived at the court of Kublai Khan at Shang-du.

Marco Polo was impressed by the wealth he found at the Mongol court. In particular, he describes "a very fine marble Palace, the rooms of which are all gilt and painted with figures of men and beasts . . . all executed with such exquisite art that you regard them with delight and astonishment." This description later inspired the English poet Coleridge to write his famous poem about Kublai Khan's "stately pleasure-dome" in Xanadu (as Marco called Shang-du).

Kublai Khan welcomed the Polos and appointed them to high posts in his administration. Unfortunately they soon discovered that this meant they were no longer free to return home. For sixteen years the Polos served Kublai Khan, traveling all over China as his ambassadors.

◀ ▼ *Two illustrations (left and bottom left) taken from a famous 15th-century French edition of Marco's story. The upper picture shows the Khan's palace at Khanbalik (today the city of Beijing). The lower shows some nomadic shepherds met by Marco on his travels. The pictures are not accurate as the artist had no pictures to follow, just Marco's descriptions.*

Finally, Kublai Khan allowed the Polos to leave China. They returned to the West by sea along the Spice Route. Their ship sailed around India to the Persian Gulf, and from here they returned to Venice, arriving home in 1295.

Three years later Marco Polo was imprisoned by Venice's rivals, the Genoese. It was during his captivity that he dictated the story of his travels to one of his fellow prisoners. This account of his travels became one of the most popular books in Medieval Europe. It was known as *Il Milione* ("The Million Lies") as few believed that his fabulous stories of the East were true. But later historians and travelers have since established that most of his tale was accurate.

▼ *A ceremonial trumpet greeting in Samarkand today. This form of welcome dates from Mongol times.*

chapter six

The Decline of Overland Trade

Did you know?

The Great Wall of China stretches nearly 1,488 miles from Gansu to the Yellow Sea. It was built to protect China from raids by the nomadic tribes to the north of the Empire. Originally constructed between the third and fourth centuries B.C. from a series of smaller fortifications, the present wall was re-built and strengthened during the Ming Dynasty, which lasted from the 14–17th centuries. This not only served to protect China, but also stood as a symbol of the Ming policy of isolation from the outside world during this period.

During the thirteenth and early fourteenth centuries, the Silk Route became increasingly popular with European traders. Marco Polo records that Italian merchants had brought ships overland along the Silk Route to the Caspian Sea, and were using them to trade along its shores. In 1340, another enterprising trader, Francesco Pegolotti, wrote *La Praticha della Mercatura (The Practice of Trade)* giving useful information for merchants setting out of the East and recommending the Eurasian Steppe Route. Pegolotti may never have traveled East himself so his guide was probably compiled from the accounts of the many traders who had.

Then, in 1368, the Mongols were finally expelled from China. Their empire, already divided, began to decline. It briefly revived under Timur the Lame, bringing great wealth to his capital, Samarkand — but then disappeared completely after his death in 1404. Trade along the Silk Route passed once more into the hands of local traders.

This breakdown in international trade was also caused by the tension between the Christian Europeans and the Muslim people of the Middle East. This was mainly due to the Crusades which the Europeans had launched from the eleventh to thirteen centuries to capture Christian sites in the Holy Land (now occupied by modern

Israel). The Christians had started taking over territory on the eastern shores of the Mediterranean, and the Muslim inhabitants counter-attacked, eventually driving them out.

In 1453, a Turkish Muslim army finally captured the last Christian stronghold in the Near East, Constantinople, and the Byzantine Empire came to an end. After this, Europeans were no long able to travel freely along the western part of the Silk Route. The remaining trade was carried on by Muslim merchants, and goods traveled between East and West by land in decreasing quantities.

By the fifteenth century, classical knowledge which was hitherto preserved in Byzantine, Sasanian and Arab libraries was making an enormous impact on Europeans. This marks the period of cultural reawakening which we know as the Renaissance (which means "re-birth"). New discoveries were being made in science and the arts, and with them came the great age of European exploration. The Europeans had realized that the world was round and dreamed of discovering a new trade route to the East, by traveling west around the globe. In 1492, Christopher Columbus set off across the Atlantic Ocean to try and reach China by this western route — and so the "New World," America, was found.

Meanwhile, Portuguese explorers such as Bartolomeu Dias and Vasco da Gama had found a sailing route around Africa and the Indian Ocean to India. This route now linked up with the Spice Route from the Far East. The Europeans had at last found a way of trading directly with China and Southeast Asia which avoided paying money to the middlemen conducting the caravans along the Silk Route.

▲ This Genoese map of the world dates from 1457. It shows the Europeans' limited knowledge about the geography of countries outside Europe. Within a few decades, this changed dramatically as the Portuguese rounded Africa and explored the Indian Ocean, and Columbus reached America.

Rediscovery of the Silk Route

Over the next coming centuries, Europe slowly extended its influence and came to dominate world trade. The Silk Route through the Middle East and central Asia was all but forgotten.

In the middle of the eighteenth century two British travelers, Robert Wood and James Dawkins, visited the site of the ancient city of Palmyra. Here, amid the wastes of the Syrian desert, they discovered the magnificent columns and ruined temples of a once-great city. It was known that this city had formerly been an important staging post on the ancient overland trading route to the East, and historical interest in the Silk Route began.

Just over a century later, the Tarim Basin began to attract interest. This unmapped region had become strategically important as it lay at the edge of three expanding empires. The Russian Empire was expanding east of the Caspian, the British Empire was expanding north from India, and the Chinese Empire was once again expanding westwards into Xinjiang (the Chinese name for the Tarim region

▲ *Aurel Stein (1862–1943), the Hungarian-born British archeologist.*

▼ *The superb ruins of the Triumphal Arch at Palmyra, from the second century* A.D.

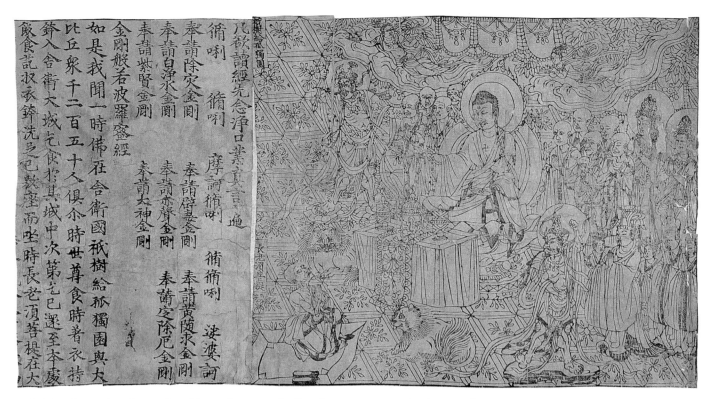

which dates back to the Han Dynasty). Explorers, some independent and some working for their country, penetrated the region and returned with stories of buried cities and treasure hidden beneath the sands of the Taklamakan.

On the evidence of these explorers' reports, Britain, France, Germany, America, and Russia all launched archeological expeditions to explore the Tarim Basin. They realized that here possibly might lie vital evidence on how East and West had been linked by the Silk Route. The Japanese too sent explorers, who hoped to discover how Buddhism had reached their country.

What the archeologists found was to exceed their wildest expectations. Digging through the sand, they uncovered the relics and treasures from the oasis cities which had once formed the essential links along the Silk Route between northwest China and the Pamir Mountains. A Buddhist culture, which few people knew had existed, was revealed. For instance, at Dunhuang the Hungarian-British explorer Sir Aurel Stein discovered a priceless collection of Buddhist manuscripts and paintings of the Tang Dynasty which had been bricked up in a cave since A.D. 1000.

The archeology of the Silk Route has continued ever since. A particularly exciting new development has been the recent use of satellites in mapping the exact course of the Silk Route, which is often visible as a worn sunken track or "hollow way." Excavations have also been carried out at important centers such as Palmyra, Ctesiphon, Merv, and Samarkand, with many of the major monuments being restored to their former glory.

▲ *The Diamond Sutra, a Tang Dynasty sacred Buddhist tract, is the oldest printed text in the world. It was found by Stein in the cave at Dunhuang.*

▼ *A figurine of a sixth-century warrior found in the sands of the Taklamakan. His armor reflects the Sasanian and Sogdian influence on this part of the Silk Route.*

▼ *Today the Silk Route travelers often pass through Urumqi in China. The pagoda above the city dates from the Tang Dynasty.*

The Silk Route Today

The trails that follow the old Silk Route still exist to this day. At the moment it is possible to travel from Xi'an (once the ancient Chinese imperial capital Changan) all the way to Istanbul (once Constantinople) — but it is by no means an easy journey. The vast majority of goods traded between East and West today are transported by sea.

A paved road exists from Xi'an at the eastern end of the Silk Route as far west as Kashgar. This remains central China's principal overland supply route to the remote western areas of Xinjiang. From here, a lorry route winds south through the Karakoram Mountains to connect China with Pakistan. This link between modern China and the Indian sub-continent has once again become an important international trading route.

The path of the ancient Silk Route west from Kashgar into western Turkestan now connects China and the Central Asian republics of the former Soviet Union. This is a rarely used and difficult route which, until recently, was closed because of bad relations between the Russians and the Chinese. Over the next few years, the newly independent republics in this area, such as Uzbekistan and Kyrgyzstan, will need to open up trade links to survive on their own and this could lead to a new Silk Route developing. As always, travel and trade along the Silk Route depends upon the tide of history.

This is particularly the case along the southern roads of the Silk Route which continue through the Middle East. The present political situation in some countries in the area has meant that parts of the ancient Silk Route remain closed for international travelers. At present, tours can follow the Eurasian Steppe Route through the old

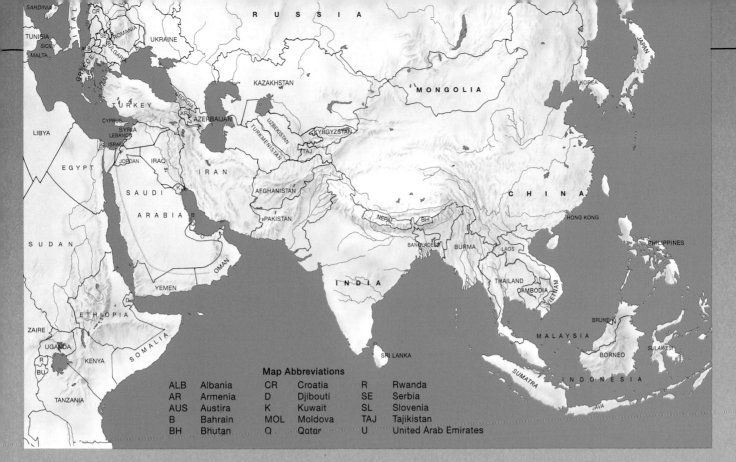

Map Abbreviations

ALB	Albania	CR	Croatia	R	Rwanda
AR	Armenia	D	Djibouti	SE	Serbia
AUS	Austira	K	Kuwait	SL	Slovenia
B	Bahrain	MOL	Moldova	TAJ	Tajikistan
BH	Bhutan	Q	Qatar	U	United Arab Emirates

Soviet Republics of central Asia, skirting north of the Caspian and crossing the Black Sea into Turkey, although it is impossible to say as yet how the breakdown of the Soviet Union will affect this area.

If international relations improve, it is possible that the entire Silk Route may one day open up again as an international overland trading link between East and West. If the road all the way from Xi'an to Istanbul became a paved modern highway, a journey which once may have taken three years could be traveled in less than two weeks. In a future era of world peace, we may yet see trucks or trains carrying international trade along the routes once traveled by Zhang Qian and Marco Polo.

▲ The map shows the countries and their borders through which the Silk Route's paths pass today.

A Silk Route Time Chart

Date	Europe	Middle East & central Asia	China & the Far East
300 B.C.–A.D. 1	**206** *Spain comes under Roman rule.* **146** *Greece comes under Roman rule.* **49** *Roman armies conquer Gaul (France).* **27** *Rome officially becomes an empire rather than a republic.*	**247** *Parthian Empire established in Iran.* **53** *Parthians defeat Romans at Carrhea.* **31** *Egypt absorbed into Roman Empire. Gives Rome access to Red Sea and Spice Route trade.*	**202** *Han Dynasty comes to power in China.* **138–119** *Zhang Qian travels to and from Ferghana.* **c.100** *End of Han campaign which leaves Chinese in control of Tarim region. Silk Route to West now open.*
1 A.D.–200	**43** *Roman invasion of Britain.* **117** *Roman Empire at its greatest extent.*	**c.1** *Buddhism begins to spread from India into Central Asia.* **30** *Death of Jesus Christ. Spread of Christianity begins.* **c.70** *Kushans establish empire in central Asia. Sogdians emerges as Silk Route traders.*	**c.10** *Xiongnu raids upset Chinese power in Tarim region.* **73–91** *Ban Chao leads a Chinese army into the Tarim Basin and defeats Xiongnu.* **c.150** *Chinese begin to convert to Buddhism in large numbers.*
201–400	**238** *Barbarian attacks on Roman Empire begin.* **330** *Capital of Roman Empire transferred to Constantinople.* **370** *Huns attack Europe.*	**224** *Sasanians oust Parthians and later take over much of Kushan Empire.* **c.250** *Sasanians control much of Spice Route trade.*	**220** *Han Dynasty ends. China splits into three.* **304** *Xiongnu invade China, causing it to fragment totally.* **399** *Fa Xian sets out for India.*
401–600	**410** *Visigoths invade Italy and Spain.* **449** *Angles and Saxons start to arrive in Britain.* **486** *Frankish kingdom, formed with land in west Germany and France.*	**531** *Sasanian Empire at its greatest extent. Silk Route flourishes in hands of Sasanians and Sogdians.*	**500s** *Nestorian Christians reach China.*
601–800	**610** *Roman Empire now focused around eastern Mediterranean. Known as Byzantine Empire.* **711** *Muslim invasion of Spain.* **793** *Viking raids on Britain begin.* **800** *Charlemagne crowned Emperor of a new Frankish Western (later Holy Roman) Empire.*	**622** *Official start of the Muslim religion.* **632** *Death of Muhammad. Muslim expansion begins.* **651** *Muslims now control Mesopotamia and Iran, along with Silk and Spice Routes.*	**624** *China reunited under the Tang Dynasty.* **643** *Xuan-Zang returns home from his pilgrimage to India.* **658** *Tang Empire at its greatest extent. Silk Route prospers.* **751** *Chinese defeated by Muslims at Talas. Tang power begins to decline.*
801–1000	**800s** *Venice established as a city state.* **956** *England unified for first time.*	**Mid-900s** *Muslim Empire divides into a series of smaller kingdoms.*	**907** *Tang Dynasty ends. Empire disintegrates.* **976** *Sung Dynasty reunites China.*
1001–1200	**c.1001** *Start of Medieval Period.* **1054** *Split between Latin (Roman Catholic) Church and Greek (Orthodox) Church.* **1066** *Norman conquest of Britain.*	**1096–99** *First Crusade - Frankish crusader states founded on eastern Mediterranean coast.* **1188** *Muslims oust the Franks from the Middle East.*	**1126** *China divided into two. Sung restricted to the south.* **1196** *Ghengis Khan becomes Mongol leader.*
1201–1400	**1234–41** *Mongols invade Russia, Poland, and Hungary.* **1245** *Friar John Carpini leaves Rome for Karakorum.* **1271** *Marco Polo sets out for the East.* **1348** *Black Death spreads throughout Europe.* **c.1400** *Renaissance period begins.*	**1248–52** *Seventh, and last, Crusade.* **1258** *Mongols sack the Muslim capital of Baghdad.* **1260** *Egyptians halt Mongol expansion into Middle East.* **1260–1368** *Pax Mongolica. Silk Route enters its last great age.*	**1206** *Mongol expansion begins.* **1227** *Death of Ghengis Khan.* **1264** *Kublai Khan founds Yuan Dynasty in China.* **1279** *Mongols finally control all of China.* **1368** *Yuan Dynasty collapses. Ming Dynasty comes to power.*
1401–1550	**1453** *Ottoman Turks capture Constantinople. Byzantine Empire collapses.* **1492** *End of Muslim rule in Spain.* **1497–99** *Vasco da Gama travels by sea around Africa to India and back to Portugal.*	**1405** *Death of Timur. Remains of Mongol Empire collapse. Silk Route trade declines.* **1498** *Vasco da Gama arrives in Calicut, India. Europeans now compete with Arabs and Iranians for Spice Route trade.*	**1405** *Chinese explore Spice Routes to India.* **c.1450** *Ming rulers adopt a defensive foreign policy and become increasingly isolated.* **1514** *Portuguese ships arrive in China for first time.*

Glossary

Alexander the Great The fourth century B.C. King of Macedonia in Greece who established an empire that stretched from Greece south to Egypt and as far east as the northern border of India.

archeology The study of history through the examination of physical remains. This is usually done by excavation or digging up historic sites, such as ancient buildings.

aromatics Sweet-smelling perfumes extracted from plant oils.

Buddhism The religion founded by Siddhartha Gautama, also known as the Buddha, meaning the enlightened one. He lived in India from about 563 to 483 B.C. Buddhists believe that a person must try to follow a spiritual path to the perfect state of nirvana, where all sufferings cease.

Byzanium The original name for Constantinople, the capital of the Eastern Roman Empire. The Empire became known as the Byzantine Empire and is often simply referred to as Byzantium.

caliphate The region ruled over by a caliph, the title given to a religious or civil rule of a Muslim city, province, or country.

caravan A group of people travelling together for security, particularly when crossing the desert or open terrain.

Coleridge An English poet (1772-1834), Samuel Taylor Coleridge. In literature, his poetry is usually associated with the Romantic movement of that time.

Constantine Roman Emperor from A.D. 310-337. He was responsible for moving the Empire's capital to Constantinople and making Christianity its official religion.

Darius Emperor of Persia (modern Iran) from 522-486 B.C. He was Darius I, one of the most able and efficient rulers of ancient Persia.

emissary Someone who is sent on a particular task or mission on behalf of another person, and often to a foreign country.

friar A member of one of several Christian monastic (as in monastery) orders, such as the Franciscans and the Dominicans.

Genoa A city and major port on the northwest coast of Italy. During the Medieval period, Genoa was an independent city-state and thrived as a center for Mediterranean trade.

Huns A nomadic people who originated from the steppe region of northern central Asia. They are thought to be the same people the Chinese knew as the Xiongnu. From the third Century B.C. onward, their warrior horsemen periodically terrorized the Chinese and the kingdoms of Central Asia. In the fourth and fifth Centuries A.D., the Huns ventured as far west as Europe and their attacks were partly responsible for the decline of Roman power.

irrigation Bringing water along specially built channels into dry land so crops can be grown there.

jade A cloudy green, semi-precious stone, often used for jewelry and carvings.

Kyrgyzstan The newly-independent central Asian republic of the Commonwealth of Independent States (formerly the Soviet Union). It is largely occupied by the Kyrgyz, a Turkic people.

Mesopotamia The fertile region between the Tigris and Euphrates rivers, which is today part of Iraq and Syria.

Ming Dynasty The ruling family in China from 1368-1644. They were responsible for establishing the tradition of an isolationist foreign policy in China.

motif A central image or figure used in art or design.

Pax Mongolica A Latin term meaning Mongolian Peace. It describes the relative peace that existed in much of Asia from 1260 to 1368 when under Mongol rule.

Persia The now out-dated name that was used for Iran. Its people, too, were known as Persians rather than Iranians. It is still used with reference to the ancient Persian Empire that existed from 550 to 330 B.C. It was ruled by the Achaemenid dynasty.

pilgrim One who travels, usually over long distances, to visit a holy place.

Pliny In this case, Pliny the Elder (c. 23-79 CE), a Roman writer. He wrote a 37-volume work, *Historia naturalis*, in which he recorded much of what was then known about geography and nature.

Sanskrit An ancient Indian language in which some of the oldest-surviving Indo-European documents are written. It was used in various forms from around 1500 B.C. to about A.D. 1100, but still survives today as the language of the Hindu scriptures.

sect In a religion, an organized group of followers holding to particular beliefs which differ in some ways from the main body of that religion.

silk the fiber produced by silk worms when they make their cocoons, which when woven together make up the silk cloth. The craft of producing silk and its cloth is known as sericulture.

Sir Aurel Stein A Hungarian-born British archeologist who, at the beginning of this century, was one of the first to uncover the lost Buddhist culture of the Tarim Basin.

Tiberius Roman Emperor from A.D. 14-37.

tax A charge on certain goods or profits from those goods made to raise money for the government of a country or region.

Tibetans The people of Tibet, currently an autonomous region of China, which lies on a plateau high in the Himalaya mountains. In the past, Tibet has been an independent country and during 7th to 9th centuries controlled part of the Tarim region.

Timur the Lame Often known as Tamerlane, Timur (1336-1405) revitalized the Mongol Empire (although he was in fact of Turkic origin) from Mongolia through to Mesopotamia, with a campaign of legendary barbarity. However, the Empire swiftly disintegrated after his death.

Turkic Specifically, the group of languages spoken by peoples of Turkey and much of central Asia, but the term is often applied to these peoples as well.

Turkmenistan A republic of the Commonwealth of Independent States (formerly the Soviet Union), on the eastern shores of the Caspian Sea, whose people are mainly Turkic in origin.

Turks Natives of Turkey, but the name is also applied to Turkic speaking people as a whole. The Turks originated in central Asia but pushed westward into Byzantine territories during the 15th century and established their own empire (known as the Ottoman Empire) through the Middle East and Balkan region.

Uzbekistan A southern republic of the Commonwealth of Independent States (formerly the Soviet Union), inhabited largely by Uzbeks, a Turkic people.

Venice A city and port on the northeast coast of Italy. During the Medieval period, it was independent and established a large trading empire.

Western Turkestan The name sometimes used to describe the region stretching west from the Pamirs to the Black Sea.

Xinjiang An autonomous region of China, focused on the Tarim Basin in the northwest. It was given its name by the Han Chinese when they first conquered the region at the start of the first century B.C.. Xinjiang means "new dominions."

Xiongnu: see Huns.

Index

Acknowledgements

The Ancient Art and Architecture Collection 27 center left and bottom; Heather Angel 19 top right and bottom right; Bibliothéque Nationale 22 bottom, 30 bottom, 36, 39 bottom left; 'The Arab Market' by J. Cruciani, Musée Crozatier, Le Puy en Velay, France/Giraudon/Bridgeman Art Library 33; British Library 31 top, 35, 41 top, 42 top, 43 top; British Museum 6 left, 11 top, 13 bottom right, 21 right, 23 left, 24 top left, 25 top and center, 26 left, 43 bottom; Peter Clayton 20/21; John Cleare 15 left, 40/41 bottom; Tor Eigeland 9 top, 10, 15 right; E. T. Archive title page, 14 top, 16 right, 31 bottom; Susan Griggs/Anthony Howard 6 right; Susan Griggs/Adam Woolfitt 11 bottom; Robert Harding Picture Library 12, 13 left, 14 bottom; Magnum/Lessing 7 bottom, 8 top, 23 right, 26 right, 38 top; Magnum/Mayer 22 top; Christine Osborne Pictures 7 top, 29 top, 42 bottom; Panos Pictures 8 bottom, 13 top right, 30 top, 32 bottom left; Spectrum 16 top; UNESCO/Earl Kowall/Silk Roads Photograph donated by the Photographer to the "Integral Study of the Silk Roads: Roads of Dialogue" 24 bottom; UNESCO/Toby Molenaar/Silk Roads Photographs taken during the Steppe Route Expedition 1991 of the 'Integral Study of the Silk Roads: Roads of Dialogue' 34, 37 top, 39 bottom right.